BLACK METHOD

Winner of the 1991 Marianne Moore Poetry Prize

The Marianne Moore Poetry Prize was established in 1991
by Helicon Nine, and will be awarded annually to a previously
unpublished manuscript selected by a distinguished poet
through a nationwide competition.

The judge for 1991 was Mona Van Duyn.

BLACK METHOD

BIFF RUSS

With an Introduction by Mona Van Duyn

HELICON NINE EDITIONS
KANSAS CITY, MISSOURI

THESE POEMS, OR VERSIONS OF THESE POEMS, ORIGINALLY APPEARED IN:

Berkeley Poetry Review: "The Possibilities of Windows";
Indiana Review: "Later, and More Slowly";
Mid-American Review: "Rodin, in Love, Unmolds His Bronze Statue of Eve";
Midwest Quarterly: "Fossils," "Pearl";
New Letters Review of Books: "Ouija, 1964";
New Voices: "Yom Ha-Shoah"–under a different title;
Northeast Journal: "A Lengthening of Days";
Outerbridge: "A Physics of Postwar Music," "Something Harder,"
"The Spring Before Your Father Leaves";
Passages North: "Healing a Dead Grandfather";
Plainsong: "For Solo Voice";
Soundings East: "Something More Common";
Stone Country: "Heirloom," "To a Small Silver Christ,"
"Uragami Tenshu Church, Nagasaki";
Wisconsin Review: "Your Father's Hands."

*Grateful acknowledgment is made to Nina Auerbach,
Stephen Dobyns, and Trish Reeves.*

Cover: Louis Marak, *After Lascaux, 1991.*
Book design by Tim Barnhart

Partial funding for this project has been provided by
the Missouri Arts Council and the Kansas Arts Commission,
state agencies; and by the N. W. Dible Foundation.

Library of Congress Catalog Number: 91-65864

ISBN 0-9627460-1-0

Printed in the United States of America
by Boelte-Hall Litho, Roeland Park, Kansas

First Edition

HELICON NINE EDITIONS • P. O. Box 22412 • Kansas City, MO 64113

*For Jim
and for Théouis*

CONTENTS

INTRODUCTION

How may I introduce this extraordinary book to its readers and yet not smother their imaginative pleasure in discovering its depths for themselves? First, perhaps, by a preparatory notice that its power is a deceptively quiet one. Reading many of the poems, feeling deeply (but quietly) moved by recognition after recognition of emotional truth, one reaches the quiet but unexpected closure and feels one's heart (quietly) turning over.

How does this poet achieve her astonishments? (Perhaps by the kind of magic physics taught by the old Jewish refugee who never mentioned his losses, who, "with his hand on its waist," first showed his very young students the open inside of the violin, then began to play, and "the sound came out of its emptiness shaped like the human body.") Certainly not by verbal pyrotechnics, nor by startling imagery. She never strains for effects outside her reach, yet the poems far outreach their apparent grounding in her controlled, clear lines, in her own "unextreme" experience. She refrains from pressing the reader for a response beyond the delicate, finely observed or imagined details she offers, and so avoids the sentimentality that, for me, often mars the poems of James Wright, who also dealt open-heartedly with human pain and losses. She has perfect emotional pitch.

Some of the poems deal with a "common" tragedy which she herself has known, the separation from a father. Imperceptibly, the loss within her own heart, her own family, falls into step, links hands in her feelings and imagination, with larger, indeed gigantic, pains and losses within the human family: those of the Indians in her ancestry, those of the massacred Jews, those of the atomic-bombed humans in two Japanese cities, and even, in a leap backwards through history, those in the "prehistoric heart" recorded by the artists of Lascaux as it tries to deal with *its* monsters. The question "What dead thing watches over the world?" asked in a poem dedicated to the children of Los Alamos, is as melodramatic as her contemplation of terrible anguish ever becomes. Remembering a childhood sight of defective fetuses in glass jars (which become symbols of those distortions of the spirit which give rise to small and great tragedies) she sees them as mistakes made with "awful ease," these "mistakes so fragile, so beautifully preserved." The word "beautifully" here is as strong an irony as she uses anywhere. Restraint, the understated, one realizes all over again, can explode with greater force than rhetorical fireworks.

For me there are three truly *transcendent* poems. The domestic one, "For Solo Voice," enters the mind of what at first seems a stock character, a middle-aged man who does not know German sitting dutifully beside his wife through a concert of Schumann lieder. But this man knows a little about Schumann; when the composer went mad he could no longer recognize his own wife and children. Feeling too ordinary to identify with a genius, he tries uneasily to dissociate himself from the vaguely remembered story. . . and yet, coming home, moved by the music, sensing the approach of old age and endings, he tries to reach out to his wife and realizes that the distance between them can never be closed since love is also a language he cannot speak. A tragic recognition, yes, but a giant step upward for the blindly struggling human spirit. The beautiful "Uragami Tenshu Church, Nagasaki" I will leave untouched, so that all readers can receive it as purely, directly and privately as I did. Of "The Way To Be Haunted" I want only to say that I don't think there is a poet anywhere who would not wish that she/he had felt and written this poem.

In the book's conclusion (as she has done, more lightly, in earlier poems) she suggests what art can do in mitigation:

> ". . . It can stop this poem here,
> in the darkest chamber of your brain
> where you look from a winter window
> into the cave of the evening sky
> and see the first star, like a way out."

Not "a way out," her truthfulness tells her as she scratches through black toward gradations of white, but "like a way out."

—Mona Van Duyn
Judge

"The *manière noire* or 'black method'
is one of the most interesting and
oldest techniques. . . . It takes its name
from the procedure in which a drawing
is scraped from a solid black image
in a series of gradations toward white."

— Garo Z. Antreasian

I
DEFINITION OF TERMS

The Possibilities of Windows

"Among traumas, the most difficult to cope with was the
removal of countless glass splinters embedded in the skin
and muscles."
—The Committee for the Compilation of Materials
on Damage Caused by the Atomic Bombs. . .
the Physical, Medical, and Social Effects

Start anywhere. Start
with the unlikely figure of Chagall
holding the small glass bodies
after the fire. Carefully,
he pieces their world together
in reds and sun yellows,
in the deep dusk blue of his own eyes.

But it is late;
already the light grows frail.
Under the translucent faces
of humans and of angels
there comes the slow release of color.
Inside them,
inside their whole bodies
begins the real night,
the noises, the smell of the river,
children asleep
in rooms as still as water.

Behind, on the sidewalk,
an ordinary pigeon bobs for crumbs,
circles, flies up,
passing quickly
under the surface of the darkening figures
so that for a moment
there is something faint in each heart with wings

and a vanishing.
Far away, in his own grandchild's room,

smoke-colored curtains move in the breeze.
The window is slightly open, like a secret
unable to keep itself.
This world is made of glass.

—Marc Chagall's *Peace* window was
inaugurated at the United Nations
building in New York in 1964.

A Physics of Postwar Music

for M.T.

I count the flights down
from the top tier of seats, down
from the old painted sky
which no longer holds.
Chips peel from plaster.
Gray patches show from blue.

The crowd moves slowly
on the stairs as the last applause
spatters like rain. This is the sound
which makes me hear it, wind
knocking against wet glass, silence
of the lesson room before we would tune, and how
you never said it, what you once lost, or
who, or that you were a Jew at all,
old man from a city called Krakow.

The first lesson was science:
you held your violin towards the light,
cupping your hand behind its waist,
showing me that (except for a small piece of wood
propped between front and back) I would see
nothing inside.

Afterwards you started to play: the sound came out
of its emptiness, shaped like the human body.

The Spring Before Your Father Leaves

At three, you do not know that your skin
holds you tighter than your father's hand
which you slip out of,
running to the edge of the river.
Your mother's words are behind you, calling.
Across the water, a blossoming tree,
whose white petals barely move.
Their small reflections
float on the surface, growing
out of the dark tree below,
the black water you're warned against. You reach down
to touch it.

Years later,
you try to tell your husband how cold, and he tries
to understand, but something has already
come between you,
something as entire,
as much yours alone
as your own skin, holding
you in.

Your Father's Hands (To the Children of the Scientists at Los Alamos, 1945)

—suggested by the work of Japanese
photographer, Eikoh Hosoe

Strange wooden fingers
point to the empty socket of the moon.
The tall lashed fences by every village
dream of themselves as human bones.
The demon Kamaitachi

waits. In a small hut
in the north of Japan, a child your own age
feels his lungs spread like terrified wings
as his mother stoops to light the darkest corner.
His father has sent them here to be safe

until the War is over.
Now, a grown man,
he is walking slowly home
along an open-windowed street
a camera against his chest. He hears
a child cry out in the night: already a light
goes on in a house.
The figure of a woman
moves like a ghost in back of the shade,
naming the monsters of this place,
lighting the corners
of another generation's dreams.
He watches her lavender shadow
rock the shadow of the child:
the tiny lungs flutter and fold
like a flying creature caught,
frozen with fear

inside the darkness of the film.
How could his camera record this scene—

or the scenes it leads him towards
through the same faint scent of japonica,
as the shadow birds of memory
skim along the ground,
swim through dark remembered paddies,
unable to lift themselves from the earth
into the dark omen, the bone-mooned night?

What dead thing
watches over the world,
watched over even Los Alamos
on certain August evenings
as women dried dishes with dusk blue hands
and men followed children into the yards?
Imagine your own beloved father
tossing you as a laughing child high, high
into the air again and again, until
in the almost imperceptibly darkening rooms,
the sweet scene begins to fade,
a snapshot on a mantelpiece.
Inside the frame, your father's kind face
is caught in a world of black and white:
he smiles at you with simple love,
as if what he and the others had made

did not change your world
and the world of all humans forever.
It complicates something inside of you—
the sight of that old family photograph—
its sky brought level, and you, at five,
nearly reaching the top of it, your arms flung wide,
face full of joy. The camera does not see
what is coming, that sudden point
when ascent turns into descent.
Your father's hands are forever reaching,
sure that they will catch you.

A Lengthening of Days

The scent of jasmine,
a half-filled cup, the memory
of your daughter's
tea-colored eyes.

Today in the garden
you speak of her death.
Tomorrow the meticulous sun
will make your shadow

promise to follow you anywhere—
away from that dazzle of first blossoms,
of daffodils, blue crocuses,
white lilacs in a jelly-jar,

on a grave. This is grief,
tugging always at your ankles,
always ahead or behind,
like a frightened child,

unable to let go.

—for Susanne Lesnik-Emas

II
FOSSILS AND IMPERATIVES

Pelvis

—*after Georgia O'Keeffe*

"It is not about death"
she said. It is about

imagination
the hard white wings
inside our bodies

the clean skulls
filled with clouds.

Heirloom

"A few remnants of the ancient tribes, now much mixed
with other peoples, remain near their old homes."
—Ruth M. Underhill, describing the eastern Algonquians

in memory of my grandfather

The hundred fingers of the apple tree
rattle in an April wind,
making the roots
dream once again
of touching your bones.
Grandfather
even the blossoms frighten me,
their skin as delicate
as the petals of your eyelids
which I touched
the day you died.

That spring,
you told me of lost rivers,
described the *monaden*
from which your ancestors
were said to have come.
You faced that ancient landscape,
no longer yours, except through the exquisite
power of desire.
When did I turn and see it—
that smallest, that most fragile
act of repossession—
the tiny world which floated on the surface of your eyes:
against your dark pupil
a blue sky opened
and birds flew deep
deep into your brain.

Instructions to an Indian Ancestor

Night pond.
The ice heals slowly
towards a dark center
closing its white skin
over the floating stars
the sky   the same sky

which tomorrow
will turn blue.
Look at me.
These are my blue eyes.

Pearl

poem for a mixed-blood grandfather

Far inland
the tree-voice
creaks in the wind.
The leaves
fall one by one
twisting
their dry fingers.
Here are the bare
branches inside you,
the thousand brown hands
curling closed,
scattered
by your breath.

Grandfather, is it wrong
to make a treasure
out of pain? Think
of a pearl.
Now imagine

my last sight of you—
dark figure walking
against the wind.
Each step
begs you
to go back.
The house
grows small behind you.

The child in the window
does not turn away,
although
you are diminished,
although
you are no bigger
than a grain of sand.

Something More Common

Nothing she can say will change
the way the play must end, has already
ended, even before she was born.
Outside the cool light loosens like hands.
Jason has left her to marry another.
Still Medea wants to touch his heart
one last time with passion.
With her own adoring fingers
she will murder their two sons.

There is nothing this extreme, this heart
rending in the actual world, and yet we are moved—
as if this story knows something more common,
would not be surprised, mama,
to open a door into a room
where you lie alone in a double bed.
You look out the open window at your world.

Tobacco fields stretch to the north, a road,
the creak of an old pulley clothesline.
A forgotten shirt fills with wind
then suddenly goes slack
like someone who has vanished.
On the distant telephone wires,
black shapes form and scatter. Even now
my words startle like birds at the thought
of how you must have felt.
Oh mama, the harm which came

not from some ancient rage
but from that simple human sadness
which grew in your heart when my father left you,

a sadness which began
deep in your body where I had once lived,
and now touched my cheek with cool fingers,
the lovesick back of a hand
which cupped itself too gently
away from my face, as if you could not
touch me any other way, half him,
the one who no longer wanted you.

Think of the way snow
pieces itself together
after its fall, lying
as you lie, beautifully cold,
to yourself,
saying that you love me

oh love me
even though I am my father's child.
My sorrow is hidden inside your own
like a child inside its mother
growing because it does not know
how to stay small, how never to be born.

Rodin, in Love, Unmolds
His Bronze Statue of Eve

The light lies inside her skin
as quietly as water.
It touches her breasts
from the inside, as if for once
she has been forgiven.

But this is the mold,
the thing to be discarded.

Something Harder

for K. Z. D.

Jenny's place has a view of the rain, huge
living room, hot afternoon, almost a year
since we've gotten together, the window
open all the way up as the three of us talk,
sip the white wine I decided to bring
instead of something harder. We feel
we will talk freely here, as if we were still
the girls we remember. But our words are
awkward, sometimes silent, my thoughts, Jenny's,
mine, Kate's, mixing with the half-learned
song which Jenny's three-year-old sings on the rug
as the rain begins to let up. No one says your name

so far, the fourth of our group in grad school.
I go to the window, lean on the sill, out past
Kate's few words about cancer, which she found out
she doesn't have, the smell of wet maples, after all,
smearing with the dampened heat, the bricks of the
building starting to dry, a single shallow pool
caught in the courtyard's sunken corner. "Were you
scared?" I say looking down. We're all afraid of feeling

a lump, or something bad, or finding a thing
that will not heal. None of us makes a motion now,
except to glance up, sip the wine, recross
a pair of legs. "I wasn't even insured," Kate says,
and I wonder if each of us thinks of you, the funny one,
wild and pretty, stuck in a hospital two springs ago,
making jokes about the drinking, about the tests,
about the handsome doctor who told you your pancreas
wouldn't hold up, that you would die if you didn't
stop. You live in L.A. with your mother now,

can't afford to come back this summer.
We all four try to stay in touch,
letters, pictures, telephone calls too late

at night and you sometimes drunk.
I keep on leaning into the air, hear
Jenny's heels in another room, the dialing of
the phone. A bird flies onto the opposite ledge
as the air begins to darken. A woman in gray
walks through the courtyard, enters a door, disappears.
I turn away from the open window and think of the year
your father died, how something in you
seemed to break. You told me you wondered where
he went. None of us knew what to do for you.

Jenny comes back, sits down to wait. She peels
an apple for her daughter who reaches out
to take it. Kate leans towards the coffee table,
putting back her wineglass now, starts another slow
conversation. Are we rehearsing, the three
of us, with you in some other place?

The Blue Letters

for F., March 1988

All the books
in your house
open on the last page
as if they know the whole story.
This is the Middle East, you say.
This is the nature of Hebrew.
For Jim and me,
your American friends,
you write in perfect English
on blue paper
the color of certain skies.
Your words must travel
to a different country.
They must be
nearly weightless.
You do not say
that today in the Gaza
outside a closed shop
a fire tugs for hours
at its black roots.
The curtains move
like pale hands, uneasy
at the open window
as you write.
You have no words, you say.
Teenagers in the occupied zones
throw stones at young soldiers
who break their hands,
their fear of each other
braided, strand over strand,

like your daughter's hair,
your youngest,
who smiles in the snapshot
which you enclose.
The children are fine, you say.
They grow.
We will not recognize them.

To a Small Silver Christ, on an Argentinian Crucifix, During the Days of the Disappeared

You throw your prayer hard at the sky
like a stone, knowing that it will come back—
that though it is a true prayer
its anger will find and punish you
on an earth which your Father constructs to turn
each day away from the light
because it cannot do otherwise,
because all its motion
is towards the darkness
of a world where you can save nothing, no one.
You are afraid that you will die,
here around this woman's neck,
she who no longer believes in you, who cannot
let you rise, as the men who have taken her son away
slam three doors.
The simple noises of kitchens
drift into the alley farther up,
two pots, a dropped glass,
the sound of wine
in a laughing voice. *Desaparecido,*
like him you will not return.

Fossils

Like vanished fingers,
the shadows of the double spires
move faintly around the cathedral,
pointing, ghost-delicate,
at the details of this earth—
the slow ticking of the iced branches,
the damaged statues along the facade,
the snow blown into the shape of vast wings

dissolving in mid-air.
Above the north portal, an angel beheaded
turns to Mary, who reaches towards him
without hands. Is it not always
these remnants which move us,
the frozen stumps
of wrists and ankles?

I stand above a case of fossils,
my face transparent on the glass.
Through my own skin
I study the stone-white bones
of the beautiful fish-lizard,
its vertebrae tossed like coins
on the bed of an extinct sea.
We with our best intentions,
our sorrows, our excruciating joys,

why should we be different?
Consider the weight of geology,
the long millions of years,
a world bearing down, impartial, on our bones,
until there is nothing left, nothing
but the ghosts of our shapes in stone.

Uragami Tenshu Church, Nagasaki

—based on a photograph by Shomei Tomatsu.
The picture shows Christian statuary thrown
on the ground by the Bomb. Jesuit missionaries
once settled in Nagasaki. The statues are of angels.

—dedicated to my niece

I address this poem
to you Angie
almost nine years old.
You have heard
that I lost my faith years ago.
You want to know if this is true.
Here is my answer:

When you think of me
remember this Japanese photograph.
One day you will learn
how it was made—
of the strangeness of art
and of the spirit.
When you do,
try to imagine Mr. Tomatsu
alone in the quiet of his darkroom.
Half way around our world
he slides his print
into the liquid.
He turns it over with careful tongs
watching the image begin to appear.
It floats like a ghost as he rocks the tray:
the angels emerge
in a flock through the dark,
reluctant like all ghosts to return
but feeling themselves drawn painfully
back, as if they cannot find their way
out of the human mind completely.

III
ELEVEN WAYS OF CROSSING

Later, and More Slowly

March 1985

A cold light gathers in the crooks of the trees, piles
quietly against the window, drifts onto the table under the
sill. Next to it, your family's piano, shipped this week from
the house in Ohio: you describe a large room, a door. You tell
me only small pieces at first. Touching the keys as if they are
cold, you play half a passage, stop. I make her up from your
few words, the old lady who did it, your mother's mother,
dead now, who showed you the thing when you were four,
her picture of nothing, clipped from some religious pamphlet.
She said it was a test of faith: "See the face," she told you.
You say you didn't want to look.

Didn't want not to. Your cousin, she said, that good boy,
had seen it right away, the face of God, where you saw only a
blank field of snow: you had been trained not to lie. You
thought of the numb smell of winter days, the way the cold
gets colder at night, flakes falling, falling, the world
disappearing.

I ask if that sorrow is still inside you? No, you say; you're
over that. You speak of our life, and your happiness, telling
me to trust what you say. Outside, a group of children shouts,
and I imagine you, small, on the walk, hearing a man and a
woman speak. The man is the one who half opens the
window. A hand pushes up, then vanishes. Inside the wife is
questioning him: she sounds to you as if she might cry, says a
few words about some poor child, but you are too young to
understand. Her husband's voice reaches towards her, turning
completely away from you. You walk away when they start to
kiss, wondering what your own life will hold. How can we
show you your sorrow will end? Look how the seasons begin
to turn. Late winter light stretches over the houses. At dusk,
the days still close like doors, but each one later, and more
slowly.

For Solo Voice

for J., at 53

Like a hand, a breeze
touches your wrist. You glance over
at your wife, shift one foot, study
the other concert-goers for any face
you might recognize. Moving
from the back of the stage, two figures
take their separate places.

A woman in blue sings movingly
in a language you can name but don't
speak: the program lists only
"Schumann lieder," which means
it might be a love song.
That's what he often wrote, sweet
Schumann, over and over,
before he went mad,

for reasons you try to remember.
Was it that he tried to drown, the music
gone bad at the end, or gone? Or
something else? He didn't recognize
anyone, his own wife, his children.
You make up each detail carefully,
a large room, the scent of flowers,
the look of certain sad faces.

Later, walking along the dusk
street, your wife slightly behind,
you wonder about them, the family
he thought was somebody else's,
the music already no more
than a sweet ghost, like this

woman, these strange children
whose names he must have felt sure
he never knew. But of course you know

this is not your own story.
You are an average person,
without madness, without particular
genius. Walking through the weakening
light, you watch the reflection
of your face passing faintly
over store windows. Men your age
begin to die: heart attacks, cancer:
you have lost one friend already.

You wish you could find some
way to explain the distance you feel
from your own wife right now, but
you have never been good with words.
You reach out a hand to touch her
sleeve, and think of the love song
you have heard, in a language
you can't speak.

Two Geese, Above Elms, Heading North

Their bones like ours
are the color of snow.
Is this the cold center
which draws them north

away from that known
land of warmth
which must slowly become
the only thing they dream of?

You lie in our bed
your eyes closed.
You wait for me to wake you.

Sweet Jim
how could we know nine years ago
that marriage moves towards
and away from its love

and once again towards?

Penelope and Ulysses

—poem to put in my husband's pocket,
before he leaves on a trip

See how the shuttle
tips under and over
under and over
like a boat on waves
of sea-green cloth.
So Penelope dreams

of far Ulysses, beloved
Ulysses. His boat
weaves the green water
rocking down and up
down and up, like a shuttle,
like a man in love.

Biology

You want your words to hold the feeling
like the glass jars themselves, unable to lie
about what's inside. But it is true
that you never intended to see them—
the deformed babies at the back of the lab—
or be with the children who snuck in
though you knew all along they might be there
and that you, little girl, would go. Down
the tile corridor, the sound of your own shoes
made you want to hide or go back. Which is how

you sometimes feel twenty years later. Like tonight—
your husband asleep, the house quiet, and you
pregnant for the first time, the thing he wants
and which you want, though you are not
always sure. It is here, into your uncertainty,
that the odd memory has come with wings
instead of arms: one of the children
thought they looked like birds, not babies.
Another said fish. Someone else called them monsters
laughing too loud by the window. The word

made you think of dark shapes on walls, and doors
closed with the best of intentions
wanting to help you sleep. You imagine yourself
as a four-year-old, frightened in that silent house
where your mother may or may not have loved you.
She did not like to say. At night you learned
to shape the darkness into creatures
which would hurt you, as she must have

learned in her own parents' silent house:

for once at this moment you can forgive her
as if you're already forgiving yourself
for any harm you may bring your own child
not yet whole inside you, as you yourself
are not yet whole, thirty years after your birth.
The image of the babies remains: you fear
that something you may do will leave your child not
fully made, in body or in heart. Which thing, or why,
you will not even know or mean.

And the awful ease of it. This is the thing
you realize, something as clear as the glass
which holds them, mistakes so fragile,
so beautifully preserved.

Errata

The baby you do not want
shrinks in your belly:
its limbs become fins
like the fish you throw back
into the sea.
Its primitive heart vanishes.
I am no bigger than the grain of rice
caught in your hair at your wedding.
The ring slips off your finger.
You are free.
You have harmed no one.
You grow younger and more beautiful each day.
You close your door
behind the young man
who is not yet my father.
On the lake
a single white sail
spreads like a wing,
startled open
like the feeling
that all will be happiness

at last.

Ouija, 1964

It is a gift.
In a house with too many secrets
you have been given
a sun and a moon at last
a yes and a no
an alphabet of your own:
here are all the letters
of all the words
that have never been said.
And you say them
with your hands.
You will become a writer.

Thinking of Theseus: Last Poem to My Father, with Regrets

Returning to his father's kingdom, Theseus neglected
to change his dark sail to a white one, a signal designed
to show that he had survived the labyrinth. The fact is
not generally known that he grew up apart from his father,
in the city of Troezen with his mother.

The hour before dawn:
a single far steeple points like a mast.
The sky falls slack against the city
the color of a dark sail.
They called to tell me you died in the night.
You never heard
what you always must have hoped I would say—
that I am all right, and in my heart, safe;
that I forgave your leaving.
Inside myself, behind my dark window
something turns becalmed. My mind moves only
towards that old story—a father waiting
for his son, a sign
that the young man has survived,
and Theseus forgetful, recalling only
the maze, and his mostly pretended
love of danger, and just too late
the light sail that must be hoisted,
the longed-for one.

Father my own sky
will soon turn white
passing first through the shades of blue
leaving nothing unsaid.

Ars Poetica Revised

The scene must slowly open
from the center
like a secret—
long silence of trees,
windless autumn river,
my own reflection
balanced
like a leaf.

Downstream the sound
of water parted
and of wings
as the geese lift startled into the sky
leaving me
faint mark below
growing smaller and smaller
until I have finally
disappeared.

Healing a Dead Grandfather

Part Indian too, I know your secret:
the wind can perch in any tree
for hours without moving. Am I right
that you are here?

Over our town
birds scatter their shadows like dry leaves
as if they could shed them this season of year,
the leaving-time.

The truth is different.
Even flying creatures
are tethered to their own dark
shapes on earth. Under earth,
you haunt your own bones.
Every year they pull you back,
the way the shadows draw their birds back down
from the huge October ghost-colored sky.

This year
as I wait for you   ·
I am afraid of what I do.
Does my love draw your shape—grandfather forgive me—
once more to earth? I give you this love
now as a gift, desiring that you
take it away from me forever.

Be dead. Be
healed of me. It is time.
Wejoo-suk, the wind is blowing.
Night has begun to fall.
Behind our town,

see how the bridge is strung over its river?
The walkway's cold railings
are shaped like flowers,
making outlines against what's below.
For anyone going over at night,
they make the water blossom

to the other shore,
one way of crossing.

The Way To Be Haunted

for M. F.

I.   Yom Ha-Shoah

They are like small children,
bringing you strange treasures,
asking hard questions, the dead.
Today they enter you like air
forcing your lungs wide open, startling them
into the shape of wings
inside your flesh. Fly.
This is the way to be haunted
by those you love. They move your eyes
towards a sky as fragile as blue glass
in which they must teach you to move
carefully, like an angel. *Kristallnacht.*
The world is easily broken.

You think of your American childhood
as if you were not safe yourself.
You cradled your sister's head
while your mother told of the gone ones,
the family's dead children, the treasures.
She spoke of separations. Parent
from child. Like the skull of an infant
your horror slowly sealed itself
filling in her silences with details
she did not tell—the red of a young girl's hair,
the scent of tea and candle wax, the sound
of a particular window breaking. Inside you,
your ghosts are as beautiful as glass.
Like family crystal
they are handed down by your mother intact.

46

Grown up now, a father yourself,
you fear their preciousness.
Carefully. Turn completely
towards their pain. Promise each beloved ghost,
as you would promise a real child,
that nothing will ever take them from you.

II.   The Gates of Hell

> Rodin chose scenes from Dante, mixing them
> with modern scenes, to illustrate the realm
> of the damned. This great unfinished work
> takes the form of sealed doors in a portal.
> After Rodin's death, the incomplete structure
> was cast in bronze, exactly as it stood.

The guard's bootsteps
move from room to room frightening
the dead children. They do not know
why you brought them here, or why
you do not take them away
now, before they think of keys.
You are yourself frightened
by certain echoes
as you look at the shining figure
on the bottom of the left-hand door,
a door which neither opens nor closes.
Your hand reaches down to touch the cold skin
of the figure of Ugolino
which feels as if it has been long dead, and yet
he is alive. You can see the pain on his face

as his fate stops forever
here, at its worst point. He is locked
in a tower where he must starve
together with his four children.
The guard's bootsteps echo, and voices.
And now, the dusk light closes
though there is no longer any tower
or key or living bones.
Only Ugolino's bronze story
which cannot move
forward. His beautiful face surprises you,
for he is one of the damned: his sins
so great that he is found
in the lowest circle of Hell. You think of the faces
of those who killed Jews. Your family's ghosts
flock wildly around you, no bigger than
your own sons and daughter. They grasp you
with terrified wings. They cannot look
away from him. They recognize evil. Ugolino's body
arches like a shield over his own small children
who are forbidden by the sculptor's dead hand
ever to finish dying. One of them
reaches out to him, but Ugolino
can do nothing to save it, nothing
to help the child escape. This is the punishment
of art: he enters the Gates of Hell forever.

And like a shriek
against your will
something in your heart
                              goes out to him,
some almost impossible fragment of mercy
through which like a door
you lead your astonished dead.

IV

Bestiary

—four French teenagers discovered the
Cave of Lascaux during WWII

i. Perhaps you will enter this poem
as the boys themselves entered the cave,
curious, hoping for treasure.
Attach a slight qualm here,
to this beginning, to lead you back—
a last backwards glimpse of the entrance
high above you like a star.
Or think of a thread.
Picture your veins unspooling
like blue thread inside your body
as you go deeper, touching the rock.

The circle of darkness in each eye
opens, like a secret. You are afraid

as if somewhere nearby you, a match
is suddenly struck: on the walls
horses are running, running

without moving. Is this their nightmare,
the human mind, in which they gallop once again
towards a single distant point of light

as you hold the lantern towards them
then frightened move away?

ii. Do you want to stop reading?
Do you want to turn this page on its hinge
like a door which opens into a room
where you are reading a different poem
involving say, the word "desire,"
and the beauties of small sorrows?

Are you afraid that if you stay,
just these three steps behind the boys,
you will soon feel, above the surface
of the earth, the slap of rails,
the boxcars thumping east,
like the heartbeats of Jews?

iii.   on the walls
        horses are running, running

        without moving

iv.   These are the things the cave people
        leave: the blood which binds
        the pigments—iron peroxide
        red, black manganese oxide,
        yellow ochre, calcite white
        like the endless snow, the endless
        fear of ice, reindeer antlers
        shaped like bare branches,
        17,000 winters, 17,000 orbits
        of the sun, each planet tethered
        to its own half-shadowed path
        by gravities so precise
        that we can barely feel them:
        feel how this cave
        reaches its hand, its three
        crooked fingers, like the fingers
        of one child born at Nagasaki,
        into the dark.

v.   Your fears
touch the walls like blind hands.
Let them move like shadows
over the horses,
reach towards the dark
vault of the rock
where they will discover
the huge and terrifying bulls, the beasts
which have thundered in both hemispheres

of our brains
since the time when we were not human.
Is this the point
at which you panic?
Imagine the hand of the ancient artist
slipping inside your hand like a glove
so that for a moment you understand
everything, here, in your fingers,
as if you yourself
had painted each creature
out of the fear that anything
might have a soul,
even the stones,
even the animals, even

we ourselves.
Close your eyes.
Hear how each step
echoes
like a stone dropped into a well?
Pretend
that you are already out.
Pretend that you are looking down

into a circle of water
in which is reflected
a blanket of clouds. The clouds
begin to part. You see for an instant
a modern city—perhaps the city
in which you live. At its heart
is the room where you are reading this poem
when the small brass wings of hinges fly open
torn from the windows
torn from the doors. The blast
slams open the sky.

vi.   "The clouds of fine particles would soon spread. . .
absorbing and scattering sunlight and thus darkening
and cooling the earth's surface. . . . temperatures
could fall rapidly—well below freezing for months. . .
creating a 'nuclear winter'. . . . A large proportion of
humans who survive the immediate consequences. . .
would most likely die from freezing. . . ."
                    —the Vatican science committee

vii.   The hand of the ancient artist
slips inside your hand like a glove
so that for a moment you understand

everything—
the reading of the oracle bones, the rustle
of lost voices, the necklaces of teeth.
This is the prehistoric heart
from which your heart is minutely evolved
so that in entering the cave

you recognize it as your own, its wild
walls, its dead passages, its beasts
which flicker on the walls
even as they do in the world of our own children
who cry out at night and are comforted
though they hear for a lifetime
the cold wind blowing in their blood,
the glaciers, the glaciers,
the spells against the ice,
the cold which has never left the heart
though every year
the skies melt
the birds wheel
like a lost language.
This is what we have done.

Let the ancient hand inside your hand
reach towards the high vault of the rock, which curves
like the vault of the human brain,
and with the blackest black,
let it stop the charging beast forever. This

is what art can do.
It can stop anything anywhere.
It can stop this poem here,
in the darkest chamber of your brain
where you look from a winter window
into the cave of the evening sky
and see the first star, like a way out.